Copenhagen exudes a ki[...] cities envious. Compact [...] the Danish capital is a ver[...] from world-class museu[...] and Michelin-starred restaurants. With pockets of nature, cobbled pedestrian streets and rainbow-hued houses, Copenhagen offers a low-key yet stimulating urban experience.

CITIx60: Copenhagen explores the Danish capital through the eyes of 60 stars from the city's creative scene. Together, they take you on a journey through the best in architecture, art spaces, shopping, cuisine and entertainment. This guide will lead you on an authentic tour of Copenhagen that gets to the heart of what locals love most about their city.

Contents

Before You Go

BASIC INFO

Currency
Danish Krone (DKK/kr)
Exchange rate: US$1 : kr 6.8 / €1 : kr 7.5

Time zone
GMT +1
DST +2

DST begins at 0200 (local time) on the last Sunday of March and ends at 0300 (local time) on the last Sunday of October.

Dialling
International calling: +45

Weather (avg. temperature range)
Spring (Mar–May): –1–15°C / 30–59°F
Summer (Jun–Aug): 11–20°C / 52–68°F
Autumn (Sep–Nov): 3–17°C / 37–63°F
Winter (Dec–Feb): –2–4°C / 28–39°F

USEFUL WEBSITES

Updates on Copenhagen's Cycle Super Highway
www.supercykelstier.dk

Public transport news and journey planner
www.journeyplanner.dk

Tax free shopping guide & refund calculator
www.globalblue.com
www.taxfreeworldwide.com/denmark

EMERGENCY CALLS

Ambulance, fire or police
112

Hospital admission
1813

Embassies
France	+45 3367 0100
Germany	+45 3545 9900
Sweden	+45 3336 0370
Netherlands	+45 3370 7200
UK	+45 3544 5200
US	+45 3341 7100

AIRPORT EXPRESS TRANSFER

Københavns Lufthavn <–> Nørreport (Metro M2)
Trains / Journey: every 4–20 mins / 17 mins
From Lufthavnen or Nørreport – 24 hrs
One-way: kr 36
intl.m.dk

Københavns Lufthavn <–> Nørreport (Bus 5A)
Buses / Journey: every 3–10 mins / 42–47 mins
From Lufthavnen (Ellehammersvej) or
Nørreport (Frederiksborggade) – 24 hrs
One-way: kr 36
www.moviatrafik.dk (DA only)

PUBLIC TRANSPORT IN COPENHAGEN

Metro
Bus
DSB (S-train, Regional & InterCity trains)
Lokalbanen
Harbour bus
Taxi

Means of Payment
Credit cards
Rejsekortet (with a permanent local address only)
Cash

Single-journey tickets allow unlimited rides on the metro, buses and trains for 1–2 hours dependent on the ticket type. Bikes can board the train with a valid bike ticket except 7–9am and 3.30–5.30pm daily from September to May.

PUBLIC HOLIDAYS

January	1 New Year's Day
March/April	Maundy Thursday, Good Friday, Easter Monday
April/May	General Prayer Day, Ascension Day, Whit Monday
June	5 Constitution Day
December	24 Christmas Eve, 25 Christmas Day, 26 Boxing Day

Galleries and museums are likely to be closed on Mondays and around Christmas and new year's day. Shops generally close on public holidays.

FESTIVALS / EVENTS

January
Northmodern Furniture & Lifestyle Trade Show
www.northmodern.com

February
Frost Festival
frostfestival.dk
Copenhagen Fashion Week (Also in August)
www.copenhagenfashionweek.com

March
Copenhagen Architecture Festival
copenhagenarchitecturefestival.com
CPH:DOX
cphdox.dk

April
CPH PIX
www.cphpix.dk
One Thousand Books
onethousandbooks.org

June
Copenhagen Photo Festival
FB: Copenhagen Photo Festival
Distortion
www.cphdistortion.dk

August
Biennale for Craft and Design
www.biennalen.dk
CHART Art Fair
chartartfair.com
Strøm
www.stromcph.dk
Art Copenhagen (or September)
www.artcopenhagen.dk

September
BUSTER
www.buster.dk
Golden Days Festival
www.goldendays.dk

Event days vary by year. Please check for updates online.

UNUSUAL OUTINGS

Nordic Noir Tours
nordicnoirtours.com

Bike Tours by The Danish Architecture Centre
www.dac.dk

Kayak Republic
kayakrepublic.dk

Cph:cool
www.cphcool.dk

SMARTPHONE APP

Find, rent and unlock bikes
Donkey Republic

Journey planner for public transport
Rejseplanen

Keeping up with the royals
Kongehuset

Practical info for CPH card users
Copenhagen City Card

REGULAR EXPENSES

Domestic letters / international airmail
kr 8-19

Cappuccino
kr 38

Gratuities
At restaurants: 5-10% for good service

Count to 10

What makes Copenhagen so special?

Illustrations by Guillaume Kashima aka Funny Fun

Copenhagen is a "slow-paced" city, with its residents enjoying everything on offer. Treat yourself to functional yet stylish clothing, explore the eclectic art scene, enjoy a cup of expertly roasted coffee or book a table at one of city's many famed restaurants. Whether you're here for a day or week, see what Copenhagen's creative class consider an essential to-do list.

1

Architecture

Copenhagen Airport
by Danielsen Architecture

Den Blå Planet (#2)
by 3XN

Dansk Jødisk Museum
by Daniel Libeskind

Grundtvigs Kirke (#9)
by Peder Vilhelm Jensen-Klint

Operaen, Winghouse
by Henning Larsen

Den Sorte Diamant, Krystallen
by Schmidt Hammer Lassen

Museet for Søfart (#3), 8 Tallet
by BIG

VM Bjerget
by BIG + JDS

2

Parks & Nature

Tivoli
Hippy theme park built in 1843
www.tivoli.dk

Amager Strandpark
Beach park for sports & relaxation
www.amager-strand.dk

Hareskoven
Former royal hunting ground
perfect for mountainbiking
www.kobenhavnergron.dk

Fælledparken Skatepark
4,500m² modern skatepark
Edel Sauntes Allé 3, 2100

Superkilen (#23)
Artists-led urban park project

Kulturcentret Assistens
Celebrity graveyard packed with
Cultural treasury
assistens.dk

3

Sea Baths
& Harbour Baths

Kastrup Søbad
(Jun 1–Sep 15)
Strandvej 301, 2770

Helgoland
(Jun 23–Aug 31)
Øresundsstien 11, 2300

Dragør Søbad
(May 1–August 31)
Batterivej 15, Dragør

Havnebadet Fisketorvet
(May 15–Sep 15)
Kalvebod Brygge 55, 1560

Havnebadet Islands Brygge
(May 15–Sep 15)
Islands Brygge 7, 2300

Kalvebod Bølge (#4)
(May 15–Sep 15)
Kalvebod Brygge, 1560

4

Bike Routes
& Shops

Den Grønne Sti (the Green Path)
A highway running along a defunct
railway through Frederiksberg

Cykelslangen & Cirkelbroen (#1)
Bike bridges bound by
contemporary architecture

Bycyklen
Copenhagen & Frederiksberg
bike sharing system
bycyklen.dk

Baisikeli
Bike rental & shop as aid agency
for African countries
baisikeli.dk

Sögreni
Modern bike & accessory design
sogrenibikes.com

Christiania Bikes
Danish cargobike manufacturer
www.christianiabikes.com

5

Art Spaces

Hall of Fame Sydhavnen
Legal graffiti wall
www.legal-walls.net

V1 Gallery
Hip art gallery
www.v1gallery.com

Charlottenborg
Beautiful art space with a nice
bookshop & café
www.charlottenborg.dk

Cisternerne @Søndermarken
Underground reservoir turned
modern glass art museum
www.cisternerne.dk

Faurschou Foundation
privately owned art institution
www.faurschou.com

Designmuseum Danmark
Design exhibitions & classic library
designmuseum.dk

6

Performance Venues

Culture Box
World class underground
electronic music destination
FB: Culture Box

Refshaleøen (#52)
Happening revitalised industrial
district

Huset
Culture house for music, film
& theatre since 1970
huset-kbh.dk

Dansehallerne
Nordic contemporary dance hub
www.dansehallerne.dk

Republique
Adventurous theatre
republique.dk

Østre Gasværk Teater
Theatre in a converted gas tank
www.gasvaerket.dk

7

Rest & Relaxation

Dronning Louises Bro
Bewildering views over the lakes,
sunset, music, beer & people watch

Sofiebadet
Book a treatment at
the historical public bath
sofiebadet.dk

Kayak Republic / Goboat
Explore the city and contemporary
architecture from water level
kayakrepublic.dk / goboat.dk

Kalvebod Fælled
Amazing sunsets, horseback
riding & lots of foraging possibilities
a short walk from
Vestamager Station

8

Copenhagen Staples

Specialty coffee
Democratic Coffee,
FB: Democratic Coffee
The Coffee Collective,
coffeecollective.dk

Hotdog & Cocio (chocolate milk)
Organic dogs: DØP by Rundetårn
Gourmet editions: *Copenhagen Street Food (#43)*
Old-school style: hotdog stands in Torvehallerne or Papirøen

Craft beer, coffee & magazines
KIHOSKH, *www.kihoskh.dk*

First-rate takeaway pizza
Itzi Pitzi, *www.itzipitzipizza.dk*

Tacos by ex-Noma pastry chef
Hija de Sanchez
www.hijadesanchez.dk

Yucatan Tacos
Yuca Taco Truck, *www.yucataco.dk*

9

Smørrebrød (Open Sandwiches)

To pair with pickled herrings
Schønnemann
www.restaurantschonnemann.dk

A classic taste
Told & Snaps
www.toldogsnaps.dk

A modern take
Aamans
www.aamanns.dk

An authentic go
Slotskælderen Hos Gitte Kik (#44)

Seasonal produce matched with in-house draft beers
Øl & Brød by Mikkeller
ologbrod.com

10

Danish Fashion & Lifestyle

Vintage eyewear
Time's Up Vintage
www.timesupshop.com

Multi-brands urban wear shop
Wood Wood
www.woodwood.dk

Cutting edge interior products
Stilleben
stilleben.dk

New & classic Danish furniture
HAY HOUSE (#25)
www.hay.dk

Flora cups
Royal Copenhagen flagship store
www.royalcopenhagen.com

Blue Fluted Plain
Finders Keepers market
finderskeepers.dk

Icon Index

 Opening hours   Admission

 Address   Facebook

 Contact   Website

Remarks

 Scan QR codes to access Google Maps and discover the area around each destination. Internet connection required.

60x60

60 Local Creatives x 60 Hotspots

From vast cityscapes to the tiniest glimpses of everyday exchange, there is much to provoke one's imagination. 60x60 points you to 60 haunts where 60 arbiters of taste develop their good taste.

Landmarks & Architecture — SPOTS · 01 – 12 📍

With majestic museums and a new, iconic skyline designed by Denmark's finest architects, there's enough for a few days of urban discovery, whether you choose to bike or ride a boat.

Cultural & Art Spaces — SPOTS · 13 – 24 📍

Hidden in and amongst large industrial buildings and in the back streets of the city centre, there's always an opening somewhere and a great museum to escape to on a rainy day.

Markets & Shops — SPOTS · 25 – 36 📍

Whether you're into shopping local food, trendy clothes, books, art prints or home accessories, there's plenty to discover. Get your wallets ready. It's all here!

Restaurants & Cafés — SPOTS · 37 – 48 📍

Vegetarians, seafood junkies, coffee nuts — you're in for a treat! The city offers something for all tastes, cooked by some of the world's best chefs. Come hungry!

Nightlife — SPOTS · 49 – 60 📍

Low-key bars, micro-breweries and late-night clubbing — there's always something to match your mood. Dress casual and go mingle with locals. The Danes know how to have a good time!

Landmarks & Architecture

Majestic museums, a freetown, bike lanes and harbour baths

Copenhagen prides itself on bikes, park life, iconic architecture and bridges. With a municipal government that works hard to create the perfect city for transportation on two wheels, cycling is the only way to fully explore what Copenhagen has to offer, no matter the season. Be sure to check out Cykelslangen and Cirkelbroen (#1), two iconic addition to the city's fast-growing super bikeway network expected to comprise a total of 28 routes.

This small capital is actually composed of several natural and artificial islands which are slowly being developed into new urban and recreational areas one by one. Board a harbour bus to go island-hopping. Starting from the black granite-clad Royal Library (The Black Diamond) by Schmidt Hammer Lassen Architects, you'll pass by Islands Brygge, the famous harbour baths, the Knippel bridge, the idyllic Christianshavn district and The Little Mermaid, where the tour ends. From there, on the 30-minute walk around Kastellet, the star-shaped fortress built to protect the city against the Swedes in the early 1600s, you will get a view at St. Alban's Church, the Gefion Fountain and the unmistakable Copenhagen Opera house.

The island of Amager also offers plenty of opportunities for archi-touring. In Ørestad, you will find the famed residential projects VM Bjerget (*Ørestads Boulevard 55, 2300*) and 8 Tallet (*Richard Mortensens Vej, 2300*) by BIG. From here, walk back to the city on Amager Fælled, a protected field consisting of reclaimed seabed and former islets, giving you a perfect break from the urban landscape.

Rent a bike at Baisekeli (*baisikeli.dk*), where you can find the famous Christania cargo bikes for families.

Margrethe Odgaard
Textile designer

Margrethe Odgaard's work spans from fashion to interior design. She has designed products for Danish and international clients such as Hay, IKEA, MUUTO and Georg Jensen Damask.

Den Blå Planet
P.016

PUTPUT
Artist duo

Swiss-Danish duo Stephan Friedli and Ulrik Martin Larsen make up PUTPUT, working at the busy junction of art photography, design, sculpture and publishing.

WAAITT
Multidisciplinary design studio

Set up in 2011 by Anders Rimhoff, Jess Jensen and Dennis Müller, WAAITT creates identities, editorial design, motion graphics and music for clients from cultural and fashion fields worldwide.

Cykelslangen, Cirkelbroen
P.014

Museet for Søfart
P.018

Makers With Agendas
Product design studio

Compact design, functionality, ease of transport, raw materials and gender neutrality make up MWA's DNA. At MWA we strive to create things the way we believe they should be.

Christiania
P.021

Mette Helbæk
Owner & chef, CleanSimpleLocal

I am also a food writer and food stylist for Scandinavian and international magazines and newspapers. I run restaurant Stedsans – CleanSimpleLocal at rooftop farm ØsterGRO.

Pettersen & Hein
Art & design collective

Pettersen & Hein is a collaboration between designer Lea Hein and artist Magnus Pettersen, who together push the boundaries between design and art.

Kalvebod Bølge
P.020

J.C. Jacobsens Have
P.022

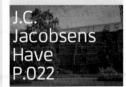

Morten Windelev
Founder, Re-public

A Copenhagen dweller for 27 years, I'm passionate about art, furniture and dining. I love that there's always something new in the city, like festival Distortion and the opening up of the waterfront.

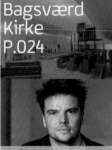

Bagsværd Kirke P.024

Bjarke Ingels
Founder, Bjarke Ingels Group

Bjarke Ingels started BIG in 2005 after co-founding PLOT Architects and working at OMA, Rotterdam. BIG's designs are known for its social, economic and ecological balance and technical innovation.

Trine Wackerhausen
Founder, Wackerhaus

I've been designing for womenswear label Wackerhaus since 2003. I have lived in cities like Stockholm and Saigon, but Copenhagen is where my heart lies.

Dronninge-gården P.023

Grundtvigs Kirke P.025

Frederikke Aagaard
Architect

I share the language and knowledge of design through TV programmes, exhibitions and writing. Besides an architect, I'm also a TV host at the Danish Broadcasting Corporation.

Botanisk Have P.027

Kim Agersten
Rocket Brewing Company

I started Rocket Brewing with two great guys after a career as a chef. For me, working with beer is in many ways similar to preparing food. Creating new flavours and perfection are my passions.

Frodo Mikkelsen
Visual artist

Frodo Mikkelsen creates painting, prints and sculptures, which have been exhibited worldwide. He's a member of Danish Visual Artists (BKF) and Danish Printmakers Association.

Rundetårn P.026

Glyptoteket P.028

① Cykelslangen & Cirkelbroen
Map J&M, P.107, 108

In a city where 50 percent of residents cycle to work everyday, an elevated bike path seems like an obvious next step. Opening in 2014, *Cykelslangen* (Bicycle Snake) starts at Dybbølsbro, winding its way over the harbour to link with the highway. The 230-metre bike bridge, designed by Dissing+Weitling, is made of steel, lending it a sleek and airy appearance. Going northeast along the waterfront, you'll find *Cirkelbroen* (Circle Bridge), which allows both pedestrians and cyclists along its 40-metre long path. Designed by artist Olafur Eliasson, the bridge is composed of five circular platforms spanning the Christianshavn Canal.

🏠 Cykelslangen: Kalvebod Brygge, 1560 to Havneholmen, 1561, Cirkelbroen: Christianshavns Kanal, 1402 & 1411

"Both lanes make a wonderful short cut in the infrastructure. Try to use the bridges after sunset. They are beautifully lit during the night."

– Margrethe Odgaard

015

2 Den Blå Planet
Map S, P.109

This seaside aquarium, created by 3XN Architects in 2013, draws you in with its swirling vortex structure. Inspired by the circular motion of whirlpools, the National Aquarium Denmark, The Blue Planet is surrounded by water on all sides, simulating the experience of being immersed in the sea. Five "whirls" radiate out from the centre of the building, allowing visitors to chart their own path around the aquarium. Home to thousands of animals from hammerhead sharks and coral reef fish, to sea otters and even birds, The Blue Planet is the largest of its kind in northern Europe.

🕐 1000–2100 (M), –1700 (Tu–Su) 💲 kr 170/95
🏠 Jacob Fortlingvej 1, 2770 📞 +45 4422 2244
🔗 denblaaplanet.dk 🔗 Guided tour (60–75min): kr 5,500 (flat rate for 1–25pax, incl. entry. One-month advance booking required.

"Although we aren't exactly fans of keeping wild creatures in captivity, the giant fish tanks are undeniably impressive. Visit Amager Strandpark afterwards."
– PUTPUT

3 Museet for Søfart

Map U, P.110

Designed by BIG as a hinge between the Elsinore region's past and present, and the Kronborg Castle nearby, the Danish Maritime Museum is built underground around the old dry dock of Helsingør Shipyard, which has been artfully preserved to allow for outdoor exhibitions and events. Bridges spanning the dock lead to the museum, where the building's irregular angles and gently sloping floors make it feel like you're on board a real ship. As you descend in a spiral, you'll learn about the country's 600 years of maritime history through interactive displays, film projections and games.

🕐 1100-1700 (Tu-Su, Sep-Jun), 1000- daily (Jul-Aug) 💲 kr 110/90
🏠 Ny Kronborgvej 1, 3000
📞 +45 4921 0685 URL mfs.dk
🔗 Guided tours (60-90min): 1130-1530 (Sep-Jun), 1030- (Jul-Aug), kr 900-1200 for 30pax max, By appointment only

"Even if you're not into Danish maritime history, this is a cool place to go. Right next to it is the famous Kronborg Castle where Shakespeare's play Hamlet takes place."

– WAAITT

4 Kalvebod Bølge
Map F, P.106

This fluid piece of contemporary architecture, designed by JDS Architects in 2013, creates a softer link between the large corporate buildings and the series of landmarks further along the harbourfront, such as the Black Diamond Library. Kalvebod Waves' recreational spaces allow for walking, sunbathing, swimming or just taking a break, offering an urban alternative to the often-crowded Islands Brygge. You can also visit the office of the world's first maritime co-op gardens, Maritime Nyttehaver, dedicated to showcasing the possibilities of urban underwater eco-farming. All this is accessible by foot from the city centre within 10 minutes.

🕐 0700–1900 (M–F, May 15–Sep 15)
🏠 Kalvebod Brygge, 1560
🔗 teambade.kk.dk
🔗 GoBoat: goboat.dk

"Rent the electric motorboats next to Harbour Bath that sail on solar energy. It's one perfect way to view contemporary architecture with an aperitive."
– Makers With Agendas

5 Christiania
Map M, P.108

A free-spirited city within a city, Christiania is a self-proclaimed autonomous neighbourhood created in 1971 when squatters occupied abandoned military barracks. Despite the government's repeated attempts to shut it down, the area has grown into a hippy town made of DIY houses, lush gardens, eateries and cultural venues, noted for a relaxed policy on smoking weed (but not anything stronger). Go see the traditional part of it: have a coffee at Månefiskeren, dine at Spiseloppen or Morgenstedet for homemade vegetarian food and watch a concert at Loppen. Respect local residents' privacy and take their no-photo policy to heart, especially in Pusher Street where hash is traded illegally.

🏠 Prinsessegade, 1440
☎ +45 3295 6507
f Christiania.org
URL www.christiania.org

"Find special places around the corners of Christiania. Avoid Pusher Street. It's become a really horrible place full of masked pushers, army tents and bulldogs."

– Mette Helbæk, CleanSimpleLocal

6 J.C. Jacobsens Have
Map G, P.106

Step back in time at this hidden oasis in Carlsberg City District. Created in 1848 as a private garden for the brewery's founder, J.C. Jacobsen, the garden was designed in the romantic style to resemble a natural landscape, with its sprawling lawn, tranquil pond and small hills built using soil excavated from the brewery's cellars. As you stroll along the winding paths, take time to enjoy the diversity of plants and tree, many of them collected by Jacobsen during his trips abroad. Before leaving, check out the Hanging Gardens, a wall of brick terraces that separate the grounds from the bottling plant. Tricky to find, the garden's main entrance is on the left side of Dansehallerne.

🕒 *Dawn till dusk daily* 🏠 *Pasteursvej, 1778*

"This is both quiet and beautiful. Let you breath in the city. Some call it 'secret garden' as little know it exists or use it."

– Pettersen & Hein

⑦ Dronningegården
Map D, P.105

A well-known example of Nordic Function-
alism, this modernist residential complex
consists of four L-shaped buildings arranged
around a central square. Construction began
on the two western buildings during the WWII,
as part of a government effort to revitalise the
area, while the eastern corner was completed
15 years later in 1958. Its distinctive red brick
façade, interspersed with yellow-stone detail-
ing, and gabled roofs lend a farmhouse-like
appearance. Close to the Rosenborg Castle
Gardens, Dronningegården borders some of
the best shops and art galleries in the city, such
as Etage Projects and Tranquebar bookstore.

 🏠 Adelgade, 1304

*"The building is beautiful every time I look at it. Its
simplicity, almost apologetic look and yet
strong and distinctive."*

– Morten Windelev, Re-public

8 Bagsværd Kirke
Map X, P.110

Designed by one of Denmark's greatest architects, Bagsværd Church is one of the few structures Jørn Utzon (1918-2008) built in his home country. Though its barn-like appearance lends an inconspicuous air, the church stands in stark contrast to its counterparts built around the same time. Instead of the heavy brickwork and wood commonly found in churches from the 1970s, Utzon's design features extensive skylights and large windows spanning the entire length of the nave, which allows natural light to bounce off the all-white interior, creating a soft, optimistic atmosphere.

🕐 0900-1600 (M-F), 1130- (Sa: Apr-Oct, & Su except service hours) 🏠 Taxvej 14-16, 2880
📞 +45 4498 4141 🌐 www.bagsvaerdkirke.dk

"It's an amazing folded canopy of concrete within, sculpting the daylight as it enters the church, like rays of sunlight penetrating the clouded Scandinavian skies."

– Bjarke Ingels, BIG

9 Grundtvigs Kirke
Map Y, P.110

Built over a 20-year-period as a monument to priest and poet N. F. S. Grundtvig, the cathedral-sized church is one of Denmark's most prominent architectural works. Inspired by the poignant simplicity of Grundtvig's hymns, P. V. Jensen-Klint's design draws heavily on Gothic elements, such as pointed arches, and finds a central role for light, which streams in through the high windows, reflecting off the pale-yellow bricks to cast an air of serenity. When Jensen-Klint died in 1930, his son Kaare Klint – who is known today as the father of Danish furniture design – took over, finishing the interior of the church in 1940.

🕐 0900–1600 (M–W, F–Sa), –1800 (Th), 1200– (Su & P.H.)
🏠 På Bjerget 14B, 2400 ☎ +45 3581 5442
URL www.grundtvigskirke.dk ✐ Church closes during services and at 1pm on winter Sundays.

"A place of beauty and tranquility. Timeless and magnificent."

– Trine Wackerhausen, Wackerhaus

10 Rundetårn
Map D, P.104

This iconic 17th century tower, with its 209-metre spiral pathway, was commissioned by the flamboyant King Christian IV for stargazing. The ramp was said to be constructed this way so horses could carry up astronomic tools to the observatory and books for the university library, which was restored in 1987 and now serves as a popular gallery and concert venue. The oldest functioning observatory in Europe, the Round Tower rises above one of the main walking streets in the Latin Quarter, offering excellent views of the city.

🕑 Daily: 1000–2000, –1800 (Sep 21–May 20), The Observatory: 1800–2100 (Tu–W) 💲 kr 25/5

🏠 Købmagergade 52A, 1150

📞 +45 3373 0373 🔳 www.rundetaarn.dk

✏ Guided tour: kr 1500–2500 for 35pax max

"The most spectacular building in Copenhagen! No stairs or elevators – only a spiralling slope to get you to the top with a view over the city."

– Frederikke Aagaard

11 Botanisk Have
Map A, P.102

Located in the centre of Copenhagen, the Botanical Garden provides a tranquil escape from urban life, where you'll find 19th-century greenhouses, walking paths, lush lawns and lakes. The garden, part of the University of Copenhagen, holds the largest living plant collection in Denmark, with approximately 9,000 different plant species. Among its 27 greenhouses, the 16-metre tall Palm House stands out for its cast-iron spiral staircase. From 2009-2012, the garden underwent a massive restoration based on the original plans from 1874, but was also updated with a sustainable watering system.

🕐 *Daily: 0830–1800 (May–Sep), –1600 (Oct–Apr)*
🏠 *Main entrance: Gothersgade 130, 1353*
📞 *+45 3532 2222* 🔗 *botanik.snm.ku.dk*

"It's a classic! I enjoy taking a walk in the garden or in one of the glasshouses to gather my thoughts on a calm Sunday."

– Kim Agersten, Rocket Brewing Company

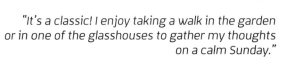

12 Glyptoteket
Map K, P.108

Created in 1888, this museum features an impressive collection of antiquities from the Mediterranean – including Egypt, Greece and Rome – as well as 19th-century French and Danish art. An avid art collector, brewing magnate Carl Jacobsen built the Glyptoteket with the goal of providing his fellow citizens with a rich cultural experience through world-renown art. After strolling among the ancient sculptures and artefacts, and revelling in works by Monet and Rodin, consider having lunch at the museum's café, set in a beautiful winter garden.

🕐 1100–1800 (Tu-W, F-Su), –2200 (Th)
💲 kr 95/50/free admission (Tu)
🏠 Dantes Plads 7, 1556 📞 +45 3341 8141
URL www.glyptoteket.com

"Love this place, so peaceful and beautiful, the architecture and the art collection is stunning! Their café is famous for cakes."

– Frodo Mikkelsen

Cultural & Art Spaces

Classic art institutions, top galleries and modernist designer house

Skip the little mermaid and other obvious tourist attractions, and go straight for the museums and galleries. The city centre offers excellent classic and contemporary art institutions, such as Glyptoteket (#12) and Thorvaldsen (#21). Around Borgergade and Bredgade, you'll find Etage Projects (#15) and Designmuseum Danmark (*designmuseum.dk*), which has a nice café and an extensive collection of Danish design icons.

In Vesterbro, the popular Meatpacking District (#49) is also home to excellent galleries, such as V1, as well as a ton of food options. A 10-minute walk away is the former brewery grounds of Carlsberg, where a "secret" garden created for the founder and his family will keep you entertained for a few hours (#6). Down the road, you'll find more gallery spaces, Nils Stærk and Nicolai Wallner, which have both settled side by side in the former garages (#18).

For international solo exhibitions and iconic design, pay a visit to the world-renowned Louisiana (#13). On the way there or back, get off at Klampenborg Station to see Finn Juhl's House (#20) at Ordrupgaard for the ultimate classic design fix. If you happen to rent a car, consider driving out to the Rudolph Tegners Museum & Sculpture Park (#22) – a perfect day trip and escape from the city. For design fairs, check out Northmodern, CHART or Art Copenhagen, which usually hold events and exhibitions open to the public. For what's going on in the city's art scene, check *www.kopenhagen.dk*.

Terkel Skou Steffensen
Co-founder, Madebywho

A product designer, I set up
Madebywho with my friend
Hans Toft. I enjoy living in
Copenhagen. It's one of the
smallest capitals in the world,
and yet one of the best.

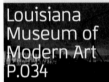

Louisiana
Museum of
Modern Art
P.034

Kunst-
foreningen
GL STRAND
P.036

Alastair Philip Wiper
Photographer & writer

A British photographer, I work
with the weird and wonderful
subjects of industry, science and
architecture, and explore the un-
intended beauty in infrastructure
and the lesser-known things.

Maria Foerlev
Owner, Etage Projects

Besides curating for my art and
design gallery and shop, Etage
Projects, I'm also a contributing writer at *The Council* and
mother of two, guided by 90%
instinct and 10% reason.

Etage
Projects
P.037

Frederik Bjerregaard
Co-founder, Moon

A seasoned fashion and lifestyle
editor, Frederik Bjerregaard
co-founded Space Magazine,
and created Moon with Martin
Giesing to produce strategic
work for lifestyle brands.

Den Hirsch-
sprungske
Samling
P.038

Christians-
borg Slot
P.039

Hvass&Hannibal
Multidisciplinary studio

Hvass&Hannibal is the brainchild
of Nan Na Hvass and Sofie Han-
nibal. Since 2006, the studio has
been creating art direction and
graphic solutions, in the digital
and physical realm.

Simon Nygaard
Creative director, Wonderland

Simon Nygaard co-founded
Wonderland with a focus on
youth culture. Today the agency
covers every part of com-
munications, from concepts and
strategy to design and execution.

Galleri Nicolai
Wallner &
Nils Stærk
P.040

Morten Halborg-Møller
Owner, Limited Works

Morten Halborg-Møller is active in both cultural and music sectors. His gallery Limited Works specialises in limited-edition art prints. He also co-owns record label Shadow Hide You.

Finn Juhls
hus
P.042

ATWTP®
Graphic design studio

Set up by Tanja Vibe and Petra Olsson Gendt in 2004, the Danish-Swedish design studio delivers simple aesthetics in graphics, product design and artwork with a feminine edge.

Mathias Høst Normark
Mathias Høst Normark Studio

Mathias Høst Normark is an explorer and enjoyer of the calm and simple Copenhagen life. He's an adept art director, formerly of digital agency Hello Monday, before striking out on his own.

Limited
Works
P.041

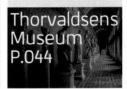

Thorvaldsens
Museum
P.044

Stefan Thorsteinsson
Partner, Studio Atlant

I'm a graphic designer and I run Studio Atlant with Cecilie Nellemann, where we focus on contemporary typographic work, including books, exhibitions and websites.

Superkilen
P.046

Claus Due
Founder, Designbolaget

I am a graphic designer and my studio Designbolget focuses on fashion, arts and cultural projects. Married with two children, I've lived in Copenhagen for 12 years and am loving it.

Sigrid Astrup
Illustrator & product designer

Born in Tromsø, Norway, I now illustrate for newspapers and run my little crafts shop in Nørrebro. With my boyfriend Kim and 5 year old daughter Edit, I feel very at home in Copenhagen.

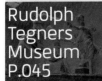

Rudolph
Tegners
Museum
P.045

Frederiksberg
Svømmehal
P.047

13 Louisiana Museum of Modern Art

Map V, P.110

Blending art, landscape and architecture, Louisiana is an immersive cultural experience. What began as a home for modern Danish art in 1958 has expanded into an international museum with a splendid collection of world-renown art, special exhibitions, concerts and lectures. Louisiana, located on the shore of Øresund Sound, is elegantly integrated into the landscape. Composed of multiple buildings connected by glass corridors, its circular shape allows visitors to stroll around the complex while admiring the views of the coast or the surrounding park, which also features a sculpture garden.

🕐 1100–2200 (Tu–F), –1800 (Sa–Su & P.H. except Dec 24–25, 31 & Jan 1) 💲 kr 115/100 🏠 Gl Strandvej 13, 3050 🌐 louisiana.dk 🎫 Guided tour (45min): kr 925 for 30pax max (excl entry). By appointment only.

"It's in my opinion the most interesting museum in Denmark, maybe in Scandinavia. Try the cakes in their café. Their 'Danish' is the best!"

– Terkel Skou Steffensen, Madebywho

14 Kunstforeningen GL STRAND
Map D, P.105

With six to eight major showcases a year featuring the latest in contemporary art, the exhibition hall's main mandate is to nurture emerging talent. Kunstforeningen GL STRAND doesn't have a permanent collection, which gives them the curatorial freedom to explore themes and ideas not found in traditional museums. The first-floor bookshop sells limited edition art books and prints while a courtyard tucked behind the building, which was beautifully designed by architect Philip de Lange in the 1750s, provides a tranquil escape from the busy streets.

🕐 1100–1700 (Tu, Th–Su), –2000 (W)   💲 kr 65/55/50   🏠 Gl. Strand 48, 1202   📞 +45 3336 0260   🔗 www.glstrand.dk   🎫 Guided tour: kr 525 (Tu–F), kr 625 (Sa–Su & P.H.), By appointment only

"*Exhibitions here are edgy enough to be in an art gallery, and classic enough to be in a museum. Stop for a coffee in the shady courtyard!*"

– Alastair Philip Wiper

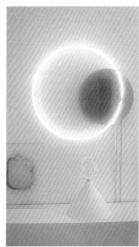

15 Etage Projects
Map D, P.105

Nestled in Copenhagen's growing arts district, Etage Projects aims to provide a different kind of gallery experience, working with multidisciplinary artists who challenge conventional art practices. Through exhibitions, lectures, workshops and publications, the gallery explores the intersection of art, design and architecture, as well as the grey area between, to create a stimulating cultural experience. From angular furniture and tube lighting to ceramic vases and stone sculptures, Etage Projects pushes the boundaries of art. Stop by Atelier September at Gothersgade 30, 1123 before or after for a coffee fix!

🕐 1100-1700 (Tu-F), 1200-1500 (Sa)
🏠 Borgergade 15E, 1300   📞 +45 2888 7786
📘 Etage Projects   🔗 www.etageprojects.com

"As I involve the exhibitors as much as I can in the shows, they turn out to be very personal. Check out the unique products at the shop in between the spaces!"

– Maria Foerlev, Etage Projects

16 **Den Hirschsprungske Samling**
Map A, P.102

Featuring Danish classical art from the 18th and early 19th century, the museum is based on the personal collection of tobacco manufacturer Heinrich Hirschsprung, who donated it to the Danish state. The neo-classical building, which opened in 1911, features small rooms, creating the intimate feeling of a private home, just as Hirschsprung aimed for. Containing more than 700 drawings, paintings and sculptures, the collection holds masterpieces from Danish artists such as P. S. Krøyer, Vilhelm Hammershøi and Christoffer Wilhelm Eckersberg.

🕐 1100–1600 (Tu–Su)
💲 kr 90/80
🏠 Stockholmsgade 20, 2100
📞 +45 3542 0336
🔗 www.hirschsprung.dk

"*It has the intimate atmosphere of a private home as opposed to the other more impressive museums.*"

– Frederik Bjerregaard, Moon

17 Christiansborg Slot

Map D, P.105

Once the home of kings and queens, Christiansborg Palace now houses the Danish Parliament, the Supreme Court and the Ministry of State. Located on the island of Slotsholmen, the building is still used by the Danish Royal Family to hold events and receive foreign diplomats. Wander to the spectacular Great Hall with its 10-metre high ceilings in the Royal Reception Rooms, where you'll find a series of tapestries commissioned for the Queen's 50th birthday in 1990. Based on drawings by artist Bjørn Nørgaard, the tapestries depict 1,000 years of Denmark's history.

🕙 *The Royal Reception Rooms: 1000–1700 daily, closes on Mondays during Oct–Apr* 💲 *kr 80/70/40*
🏠 *Prins Jørgens Gård 1, 1218* 🔗 *kongeligeslotte.dk*
🎧 *Guided tour (EN): 1500 daily*

"Go to Thorvaldsens Museum (#21) afterwards, where we shot the album cover for Efterklang's Magic Chairs in 2009."

– Hvass&Hannibal

18 Galleri Nicolai Wallner & Nils Stærk

Map G, P.106

Located on the grounds of the old Carlsberg breweries, these two galleries are housed in the same building, a 2,000-square-metre garage formerly used for beer trucks. Nicolai Wallner was the first to open in the area in 2009, conceiving of a cultural hub that would redefine the art scene in Copenhagen. Today, both galleries feature the very best in contemporary art by both Danish and international artists working in all different media, including Elmgreen & Dragset, Richard Tuttle, SUPERFLEX and Darío Escobar.

🕐 1200–1700 (Tu–F), –1500 (Sa)
🏠 Ny Carlsberg Vej 68, 1760 📞 *Galleri Nicolai Wallner*: +45 3257 0970, *Nils Stærk*: +45 3254 4562
🔗 www.nicolaiwallner.com, nilsstaerk.dk

"These two galleries are neighbours and top of the pops of Danish galleries. If you want to see high-ranking international art, you need to visit them."

– Simon Nygaard, Wonderland

19 Limited Works

Map C, P.103

Starting as an online gallery, Limited Works eventually sets up shop in Nørrebro, where they sell exclusive editions of hand-printed art starting from less than USD100. This is the place to go if you're searching for street art or the next up-and-coming talent from the Danish and international art scene. Located on Blågårdsgade, a street famous for its diversity in food, residents and amazing block parties, the gallery boutique also hosts frequent art openings and events.

🕐 1300-1730 (W-F), 1100-1500 (Sa-Su)
🏠 Blågårdsgade 17, 2200
☎ +45 6168 9844
📘 Limited Works
🔗 www.limitedworks.com

"My take on a modern art shop. Monday and Tuesday are normally closed but can be opened by appointment at hello@limitedworks.com."

– Morten Halborg-Møller, Limited Works

20 Finn Juhls hus
Map W, P.110

Built in 1942 just north of Copenhagen, the home of architect and furniture designer Finn Juhl embodies his philosophy of designing "from the inside out," starting with the furniture, which he believed determined the overall architectural character of any building. An early example of open-plan design, the house features its original interior, filled with Juhl's personal collection of Modernist art and white-walled rooms that glow when light from the surrounding woods streams in through the large windows. Juhl also used his home to test furniture, such as his iconic Fj45 and Fj46 chairs, before scaling it up.

🕐 1100–1645 (Sa–Su & P.H.)
🏠 Kratvænget 15, 2920
📞 +45 3964 1183
URL ordrupgaard.dk/finn-juhls-hus

"Here you get to experience some of the nature outside Copenhagen. It's not far away from the sea which is also worth visiting."

– Mathias Høst Normark, Mathias Høst Normark Studio

21 Thorvaldsens Museum
Map D, P.105

Opening in 1848, the museum was created to house the work of Danish sculptor Bertel Thorvaldsen, who spent most of his career in Rome. Located beside Christiansborg Palace, the majestic building is covered in vivid hues, from the bright walls and mosaic floors to the tiled ceiling, creating a colourful backdrop for Thorvaldsen's marble and plaster sculptures. Take a rest in the courtyard, where the artist is buried, and check out the frieze on the outside, which depicts Thorvaldsen's return in 1838.

🕐 1000–1700 (Tu–Su) 💲 kr 50/free admission (W)
🏠 Bertel Thorvaldsens Plads 2, 1213
📞 +45 3332 1532 URL www.thorvaldsensmuseum.dk
🔗 Private guided tour (EN/DE/DA): kr 695 (flat rate for 25pax max.) By appointment only

"Its impressive sculptures, the interior's colours and all wonderful create a timeless atmosphere. Go there for a break on a rainy day. Bring your sketchbook and enjoy."
– ATWTP®

22 Rudolph Tegners Museum
Map T, P.110

Designed by the Danish artist himself in the 1930s to showcase his work, Rudolph Tegner Museum stands distinctively like a bunker in the hilly countryside on Zealand's north coast. In contrast to the prevailing neo-classicalist ideals of the time, Tegner (1873-1950) emphasised intensity and monumental forms in his sculptures, traits that are readily apparent in the concrete colossus. Housing over 200 pieces of Tegner's art, which are also on display in the outdoor sculpture park, the museum stands as a testament to one artist's determination and vision for a lasting legacy. Both Tegner and his wife were buried in the grounds underneath the museum's central hall.

🕐 Tu-Su: 1200-1700 (Apr 15-May, Sep-last Sunday of school holidays in Oct), 1100-1800 (Jun-Aug)
💲 kr 50/40 🏠 Museumsvej 19, 3120
📞 +45 4971 9177 🔳 www.rudolphtegner.dk
🔗 Monthly guided tour (EN/IT/RU/DA): kr 675 (excl. entry), By appointment only

*"The amazing sculpture park can be entered free.
Take a walk!"*
– Stefan Thorsteinsson, Studio Atlant

23 Superkilen
Map P, P.109

This 750-metre long public park in Mimersgade weaves through Nørrebro, one of the most ethnically diverse neighbourhoods in Copenhagen. Reflecting the multiculturalism of its surroundings, Superkilen is filled with over 100 objects nominated by local residents, including a fountain from Morocco, an octopus sculpture from Japan and neon signs from Qatar. The park was co-developed by architectural firms BIG and Topotek1, and artist group SUPERFLEX, featuring three colour zones, namely Red Square for cultural activities, Black Market for social gatherings and Green Park for sports and games.

🏠 Nørrebroruten, 2200
f Superkilen URL superkilen.dk

"Get the Superkilen app. It has a very good map of the park and interesting texts about the contributing artists and their artworks. A must have if you're visiting."

– Claus Due, Designbolaget

24 Frederiksberg Svømmehal
Map Q, P.109

This public pool and bathhouse, with its luxury department and spa, is becoming an increasingly popular place for rest and relaxation. Experience weightlessness in the saltwater pool, take a soothing dip in a Jacuzzi or unwind in the sauna with some aromatherapy. One of the oldest in the country, Frederiksberg Svømmehal was designed by architect A. S. Lauritzen in the 1930s and features five halls with original mosaics by Danish painter Vilhelm Lundstrøm.

🕐 Pool: 0700–2030 (M–F), –1530 (Sa), 0800–1530 (Su), 0900–1530 (P.H. except Dec 24–26, 31 & Jan 1), Spa: 1100–2030 (M–F), 0900–1530 (Sa–Su & P.H.)
💲 Pool: kr 42/20, Spa: kr 165 (incl. access to pool)
🏠 Helgesvej 29, 2000 📞 +45 3814 0400
🌐 svoemmehal.frederiksberg.dk
🖇 Spa: 15+, Last entry: 30min before closing

"There is amazing 'saunagus (steam bath with herbs)' every hour and the staff here are Danish champions. Reserve time for the salt lemon scrub after spa."

– Sigrid Astrup

Markets & Shops

Danish design, minimalistic fashion and busy food markets

In contrast to just a few years ago, Copenhagen's design scene today is much more varied and complex. While international media still mainly focus on the major design icons of the golden age in the 50's and 60's, new brands, collaborations and shops are popping up, with some starting to make a name for themselves.

Stay off the main walking street, unless you're going to contemporary-furniture store HAY HOUSE (#37). The side streets are where you'll discover the "hidden" gems and local favourites, such as Sing Tehus (#34), Cinnober (#28), Henrik Vibskov Boutique (#31) and Norse Projects (#32) – all located in the city centre. In Vesterbro, your first stop should be the Meatpacking District (#49), where you'll find Nibble shop specialising in food publications. In Østerbro, pick up a cookie or pastry from Leckerbaer (*leckerbaer.dk*) or head over to indoor flea market at Remisen (*Blegdamsvej 132, 2100*) for some great vintage shopping and old jazz records. Nørrebro, in particular, is becoming a top destination for design, vintage goods and art, as its diverse population attracts trendy shops and eateries.

Design, Craft and Food markets always seem to be going on somewhere in the city. Look out for Finders Keepers (*finderskeepers.dk*) events or the bi-annual Blickfang fair to grab something unique and handmade (*www.blickfang.com*).

Anders Arhoj
Graphic designer

I explore the relationship between Scandinavian simplicity and traditional Japanese culture through interior products and ceramics that I make at my little studio near the harbourfront.

Carina Juul
Founder, WDV STUDIO

I'm the creative director of WDV STUDIO, where we shape visual identities and create strategic design solutions across all media.

Pernille Snedker Hansen
Founder, Snedker Studio

I handcraft wood surfaces with a unique marbling technique for interiors, furniture and artworks. Copenhagen's fresh air, vibrant culture and seawater in winter keep me creatively energised.

Norm Architects
Architecture studio

Since 2008, Norm has worked on residential architecture, commercial interiors, industrial design and art direction, with a focus on quality and timelessness.

Rasmus Drucker Ibfelt
Co-founder, e-Types & Playtype

Rasmus Drucker Ibfelt is the creative director and partner of design agency e-Types and brand Playtype. He now lives in Frederiksberg with his wife and two kids, Herbert and Villum.

Martin Garde Abildgaard
Film director

Martin Garde Abildgaard has directed commercials for BMW and Adidas, and music videos. He also runs art project "America" that combines film and photography with music and fashion.

Henrik Vibskov
Fashion designer

Henrik Vibskov regularly explores the fields of music, art and interior design, in addition to fashion. His collections have been shown at Paris Men's Fashion Week, MoMA and Palais de Tokyo.

Henrik Vibskov Boutique P.059

Norse Store P.060

Jesper Elg
Founder, V1 Gallery

Jesper Elg is the director of V1 Gallery, currently living in Vesterbro, Copenhagen.

Barbara í Gongini
Fashion designer

Also an active participant in the Nordic and international art discourse, Barbara í Gongini launched her namesake brand in 2005 to promote sustainable avant-garde clothing design.

Maria Black Jewellery P.061

Thomas Ibsen
Please wait to be seated

I'm a photographer turned furniture designer, outgoing and well-informed about the art and music scenes. Also an avid traveller, I enjoy finding small hidden secrets wherever I go.

Sing Tehus P.062

Pisserenden P.063

Ninna York
Founder, Ninna York Jewellery

I'm a jewellery designer and opened my store with a good friend, Josefine Smith. My creations are handmade, usually with silver and increasingly with gold and diamonds.

Carla Cammilla Hjort
Entrepreneur

As the creator of Rebel Agency, ArtRebels.com and Trailerpark Festival, I strive to drive positive change via co-creation and bridge the gap between creative talents and corporations.

Torvehallerne P.064

25 HAY HOUSE
Map D, P.105

A Mecca for minimalist-design lovers, HAY's shop in central Copenhagen has become a "must visit" since opening in 2008. An international brand and manufacturer itself inspired by the innovative simplicity of 1950s and 1960s Danish design, HAY specialises in functional products with clean lines and unique shapes, all to be found in the 500-square-metre boutique. On two floors, the loft-like space is laden with Hay's own collection of contemporary furniture and decor accessories. Highlights are rugs, vases and pillows, as well a coveted line of stationery and quirky toys which style-savvy trippers should not miss.

🕐 1000–1800 (M–F), –1700 (Sa), 1200–(monthly 1st Su)
🏠 2–3/F, Østergade 61, 1100
📞 +45 4282 0820
URL www.hay.dk

"*HAY mainly sells their own products and has many to offer! It's a perfect place to find small, affordable designer souvenirs for your friends.*"

– Anders Arhoj

26 Schäfer Grafisk Værksted
Map D, P.104

Amazing craftsmanship and art are what you can expect from this local gallery, where owner Michael Schäfer also runs his graphic workshop. Tucked into a basement, visitors will find art books and journals, as well a variety of signed and limited prints on display, including linocut, silkscreen, copperplate and woodcut from Danish artists like Michael Kvium and Asbjørn Skou Armsrock. Afterwards, consider having lunch at nearby Berkeley Take Away, which serves authentic US-style fried chicken sandwiches done to perfection and excellent homemade lemonade.

🕐 0930–1730 (M–F), 1000–1300 (Sa)
🏠 Nansensgade 43, 1366
📞 +45 3313 1231
URL schaefergrafik.dk

"If you're interested in the visual arts, this is a great opportunity to pick up a unique souvenir."
– Carina Juul, WDV STUDIO

27 **Format Artspace**
Map D, P.104

Opening in 2013, Format Artspace focuses on working with Danish artists who have attracted international attention. Bi-monthly exhibitions and show openings showcase art that experiments with medium and material, whether it be graphics, textiles, 3D prints, cartoons or paintings. Located on Nansensgade, a cosy street with a great variety of wine bars and cafés, the gallery also features a wide selection of fine-art prints for sale, collaborating with printers specialising in etching, lithography and serigraphy.

🕐 1200–1700 (Tu–F), 1100–1500 (Sa) & by appointment
🏠 Nansensgade 35, 1366
📞 +45 6168 7844
🔗 www.formatartspace.dk

"Go there to explore a great variety of beautiful and affordable artwork on paper by works by many great local artists!"

– Pernille Snedker Hansen, Snedker Studio

28 Cinnober
Map D, P.104

An independent bookshop hidden in the basement of an old building across from the Rundetårn Tower, Cinnober features a handpicked selection of international, visually inspiring books on art, graphic design, illustration, architecture, street art, fashion and industrial design. The owner, who travels frequently to fairs around the world, is great at selecting clever writing tools and stationery you won't find elsewhere, keeping the store's amazing selection well stocked. Muji fans will love this shop!

🕐 1100–1730 (M–F), –1500 (Sa)
🏠 Landemærket 9, kld. th., 1119
📞 +45 2613 9833
URL www.cinnobershop.dk

"It's a hidden little gem."
– Norm Architects

29 Playtype Store

Map H, P.107

This small shop sells typography-adorned objects, such as posters, mugs and stationery all designed by the creative agency e-Types. In 2010, the agency created its own typography foundry to showcase its work, later building a street-level store that has grown to host events and the occasional guest exhibitor, and launch collaborations. Close to the shop located on the charming street Værnedamsvej, you'll find the fishmonger, butcher and cheese shop next door to Scandinavian design and fashion, a French café and one of the city's best magazine and book shops, Thiemers Magasin on the side street – Tullinsgade.

🕙 1200–1800 (M–F), 1100–1500 (Sa)
🏠 Værnedamsvej 6, 1619 📞 +45 6040 6914
🔗 playtype.com

"From posters to mugs, there is something for everyone."

– Rasmus Drucker Ibfelt, e-Types & Playtype

30 Storm
Map D, P.105

While Paris has Colette, Copenhagen has Storm – one of the leading lifestyle and fashion stores in Europe. Beyond clothing, you'll also find music, magazines, books and in-store art exhibitions. A great source of new and cool music, the store's selection reflects owner Rasmus Storm's love of the medium. The shop is located in a great area, bordering the shopping district. Within a few minutes of walking, you can visit the royal gardens, watch a rare-movie screening at Cinemateket or check out the latest in Danish and Scandinavian design at Gubi's flagship store or Hay House.

🕐 1100–1730 (M–Th), –1900 (F), 1000–1600 (Sa)
🏠 Store Regnegade 1, 1110
📞 +45 3393 0014
🔗 stormfashion.dk

"*The owner Rasmus Storm loves music and he is really good at sourcing rare and amazingly cool music that you can't find any where else in Scandinavia.*"
– Martin Garde Abildgaard

31 Henrik Vibskov Boutique
Map D, P.104

Known for his playful and edgy approach to
women and menswear, Henrik Vibskov – a
Danish designer, artist and musician – opened
the shop in 2006, setting fashion trends ever
since. Besides Vibskov's own collections, the
boutique also features whimsical and avant
garde work from a carefully selected group of
designers, such as Stine Goya and Issey Miyake.
Next door is the main library Democratic
Coffee, which currently holds the title for the
city's best croissants. Vibskov also owns a tiny
coffee shop on Papirøen next to Copenhagen
Street Food, where his studio is located.

🕐 1100–1800 (M–Th), –1900 (F), –1700 (Sa)
🏠 Krystalgade 6, 1172
📞 +45 3314 6100
🔗 henrikvibskov.com

---

*"Just a quick getting into my universe, stuff I like, and
buy a beer. Try the toilet. Amy Winehouse also did,
and she had a hangover though."*

– Henrik Vibskov

32 Norse Store
Map D, P.105

Featuring the motto "created for life - good for all seasons", Norse Store focuses on simple, clean and functional designer clothes for men, but has recently ventured into womenswear. Besides their own bi-annual collections, they also create "Norse Projects" a series of collaborations with design-focused brands from other industries, such as the Danish textile manufacturer Kvadrat and furniture design company Fritz Hansen. If you get hooked, their webshop will keep you stocked around the globe.

🕐 1000–1800 (M–Th), –1900 (F), –1600 (Sa)
🏠 Pilestræde 41, 1112
📞 +45 3393 2626
URL www.norsestore.com

"These are clothes that you can wear everyday while surviving Copenhagen weather on a bicycle."

– Jesper Elg, V1 Gallery

33 Maria Black Jewellery
Map D, P.105

Its namesake owner launched her first collection in 2010, fusing her passion for precious metals with a modern take on jewellery design. Opening in 2013, the flagship store is the culmination of Maria Black's impressive growth story, building a distinctive brand that now counts several celebrities among its clients. Located in Silkegade, the shop's dark interior reflects the products on display: raw, edgy and refined. Go here for affordable yet elegant jewellery you can wear everyday.

🕐 1100–1800 (M–Th), –1900 (F), 1000– (Sa), –1600 (Su)
🏠 Silkegade 13, 1113
📞 +45 3311 5066
URL www.maria-black.com

"Denmark has cultivated fantastic jewellery designers and Maria Black is one of them that I recommend to visit while you're in town."

– Barbara í Gongini

34 **Sing Tehus**
Map D, P.104

A cosy and serene haven within the bustling city centre, this Japanese-inspired tea shop and café is rare spot for a bowl of expertly prepared whipped matcha. Sing Tea House specialises in Japanese green tea, but also offers a high-quality selection from other parts of the world, mainly China and Korea. If you're feeling peckish, try some of their delicate cakes or scrumptious sandwiches. The shop also hosts tea ceremonies, workshops and exhibitions ideal for a good all-round enjoyment.

🕐 1000–1730 (M–F), –1500 (Sa)
🏠 Kompagnistræde 30, 1208
📞 +45 3311 6603 📘 singtehus
🔗 singtehus.dk

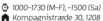

"Ask the staff for what's happening in the subcultural art scene. The owner is well informed."

– Thomas Ibsen, Please wait to be seated

35 Pisserenden
Map D, P.104

With its small crooked buildings and colourful history, the oldest area of Copenhagen feels like a small city in itself, where you'll find everything you need within a few blocks. Here, you'll see a graffiti paint shop on the same street as an organic soup restaurant and custom-made jewellery store. Snag a vintage dress or shirt for a bargain, or pick out a handmade silk kimono for your evening out. If you develop a craving for buckwheat galettes or classic brasserie dishes, dine at an authentic French restaurant, one of a small group that call the area home. For drinks at night, there are several good bars.

🏠 *Sankt Peders Stræde,*
Studiestræde & Larsbjørnsstræde
URL *www.nextdoorcafe.dk*

"*Get your coffee and breakfast at Next Door Café in Lars Bjørn Stræde and enjoy it outside in the street.*"

– Ninna York, Ninna York Jewellery

36 Torvehallerne
Map D, P.104

The first year-round fresh food market in the city, Torvehallerne boasts over 60 stalls offering everything from world-renowned coffee to confit de canard sandwiches. Selected small-scale farmers liven up the place every Wednesday with an excellent selection of fresh produce and homemade specialities. Head to Summerbird for gourmet chocolate and nice Danish delicacies at shops like Omegn and Slagter Lund. Be sure to check out the food trucks outside – one is owned by a former head chef at Noma who now serves Mexican food with incredible guests chefs.

🕐 1000-1900 (M-Th), -2000 (F), -1800 (Sa), 1100-1700 (Su), Coffee & pastries: 0700- (M-F), 0800- (Sa-Su)
🏠 Frederiksborggade 21, 1360
URL torvehallernekbh.dk

"*I love this place because I love fresh food. This is the first of its kind in Copenhagen. A great food market for food lovers.*"

– Carla Cammilla Hjort, Rebel Agency, ArtRebels.com & Trailerpark Festival

Restaurants & Cafés

Sustainable coffee roasters, new Nordic feasts and beyond

Copenhagen is a foodie's haven. With excellent chefs from all over the world travelling here to work, perhaps initially as stagiaires for Noma and other top gourmet restaurants, many of them stay behind to open up smaller and more affordable establishments. The result: a city with superb dining from across the globe and at all price points. The café scene, meanwhile, is moving away from classic brunches and towards top-quality coffee shops and excellent bakeries – go for The Coffee Collective in Frederiksberg or Alimentari (#38) at Islands Brygge across the harbour.

Good restaurants are spread all over the city, so there's bound to be something wherever you are. For the adventurous and experienced diner, book your table at Christian Puglisi's Michelin-starred Relæ (#46) in Jægerbroggade or try its "little sister" Italian eatery Bæst (#41) in Nørrebro. Most of the upscale restaurants are closed on Sundays and Mondays, so plan ahead.

In the Meatpacking District next to Fiskebaren (#42), brewers are entering the restaurant scene with the latest venture from Mikkeller (#59) and 3Floyds: Warpigs Brewpub, which serves craft beer and Texas-style barbecue. For more spontaneous food experiences, check out some of the city's great food markets, such as Kødbyens Mad og Marked, Copenhagen Street Food (#43) and Rebel Food.

Pelle Martin
Founder, Spring/Summer

I am a graphic designer, creative director and founder of digital agency Spring/Summer. Husband to Majken and father to Marley, I'm loving life in Copenhagen.

Alimentari
P.071

Bo Lindegaard & Lasse Askov *Founders, I'm a KOMBO*

I'm a KOMBO creates an innovative, sociable dining experience by marrying imagination with tasty food and craft. They offer catering, private dining and concepts for restaurants and brands.

Rebecca Uth
Creative director, RO

Rebecca Uth is the creative director of RO, which was founded in 2013. Working with select designers, she creates art objects and design rooted in a love of craftsmanship, quality and tranquility.

Kaffebar
P.070

Tranquebar
P.072

Sine Jensen
Illustrator

I'm a Danish illustrator with a MA degree from KADK. My detailed pencil drawings revolve around pop culture, usually with an ironic and humorous angle.

Bæst
P.074

Jack Dahl
Founder, Homework

I'm the creative director of Homework. Our specialties are visual brand expressions and communications created for luxury, fashion, beauty, lifestyle and cultural brands.

Josephine Philip
Vocalist, Darkness Falls

Josephine Philip is a singer and songwriter based in Copenhagen. Together with guitarist and bass player Ina Lindgreen, she forms pop-noir band Darkness Falls.

Sort Kaffe &
Vinyl
P.073

Fiskebaren
P.075

Line Rix
Managing partner, Kit Couture

Kit Couture unites fashion with crafts. I really love Copenhagen and have my base in the vibrant Vesterbro district. I'm also the co-founder of digital design agency, 1508.

Slotskælderen hos Gitte Kik
P.078

Casper Heijkenskjöld
Graphic designer

Born in Malmö, Sweden, I currently run my studio in Copenhagen. I help music, fashion and film clients achieve their goals through well-formulated visual communication.

Kim Herforth Nielsen
Founder, 3XN Architects

C.F. Hansen Medaille-winner Kim Herforth Nielsen is a Knight of the Order of the Dannebrog and chartered member of RIBA. 3XN's latest projects include the Blue Planet and Bella Sky Hotel.

Copenhagen Street Food
P.076

Café Victor
P.079

Jakob Mielcke
Partner, Mielcke & Hurtigkarl

Born in Aarhus, Denmark, Jakob Mielcke is a self-taught chef who has worked with masters such as Pierre Gagnaire. He's currently the executive chef and partner at M&H.

Kadeau
P.081

Marie Louise Munkegaard
Lifestyle photographer

I love to create portraits bathed in natural light, meet people and experience new places. I also love to eat and photograph food. Shooting for Bornholm Kadeau is the best job in the world!

Esteban
Filmmaker

I am a German filmmaker working mostly with fashion and lifestyle brands. I came to Copenhagen for its natural aesthetics and great taste. I couldn't imagine a better choice.

Relæ
P.080

Stedsans – Clean-SimpleLocal
P.082

37 Kaffebar
Map C, P.103

This coffee and wine bar by digital agency Spring/Summer may have a small menu but its focus is on quality, not quantity. Black filter coffee, a soft-boiled egg and a simple croissant are common breakfast staples here. It's a cosy, well-lit place where you'll find students and freelancers on their laptops, as well business people and shoppers taking a break. If the weather's nice, take advantage of the outdoor seating. Located in Elmegade, a fashionable and iconic street in Nørrebro, Kaffebar is close to the movie theatre Empire Bio, Acne Archives and Le Fix – a tattoo shop, fashion brand and gallery.

🕐 0800–1800 (Su–Tu), –2000 (W–Sa)
🏠 Elmegade 4, 2200
☎ +45 3535 3038
URL elmegade4.dk

"This is where we go for management meetings and a day break. Drop by during the day for a nice cup of mocha or a chilled rosé before nightfall on the street."

– Pelle Martin, Spring/Summer

38 Alimentari
Map F, P.106

A small café, take away, wine shop and deli rolled into one, Alimentari, in the Islands Brygge area, is an extension of the Italian restaurant Il Buco. Their menu is fixed but simple. For breakfast, expect small dishes served with strong black coffee and fresh juice, plus scrumptious pastries. The rest of the day, you can get freshly made sandwiches, a salad or pasta. Every Friday at 5 p.m. aperitivo, a drink served before meals, is available with an excellent wine list usually announced the day before. Be prepared to wait during weekday lunch hours as they also cater to startups nearby.

🕐 0730–1900 (M–Th), –2345 (F), 0800–2345 (Sa), –1700 (Su) 📍 Njalsgade 19C, 2300 📞 +45 3132 6811
f alimentari København URL alimentari.dk

"Kristor who owns the place is a master in hostmanship, quality and atmosphere. Don't miss Nokken, an old allotment area like Christiania but without the weed."
– Bo Lindegaard & Lasse Askov, I'm a KOMBO

39 Tranquebar
Map D, P.105

A mix between a café and a bookstore, Tranquebar is run by a former librarian who ventured into the travel industry before coming back to books. Its focus is mainly on travel literature but the store also has a great selection of antique books, cookbooks and beautifully designed books for kids. Writers and poets often hold lectures or talks at the shop, which also serves regularly as a small concert venue. If you're looking for a quiet place to hang out for a few hours, head over to the café, where you'll find cosy seating and a refined menu of food and drinks to tide over any cravings.

🕐 1000–1800 (M–F), –1600 (Sa)
🏠 Borgergade 14, 1300
📞 +45 3312 5512
🔗 www.tranquebar.net

"I have travelled a lot and in Tranquebar my memories come back."
– Rebecca Uth, Ro

40 Sort Kaffe & Vinyl
Map I, P.107

The owner's dual passion for music and coffee come together in this shop, where the staff – mainly local musicians – play records while serving you a quality cup of joe. With a fantastic selection of vinyl and pastries, this cosy café is where locals and those in the know go to hang out in Vesterbro. The café is tiny, so keep your eyes peeled, or you might miss it! If you want some fresh air, grab a seat outside and admire the view of the beautiful residential buildings lining the street. Nearby on Istedgade, there are several great vintage shops and fashion boutiques, including Kyoto.

🕐 0800–1900 (M–F), 0900– (Sa), 1000–1800 (Su)
📍 Skydebanegade 4, 1709 📞 +45 6170 3349
📘 SORT KAFFE & VINYL

"This is my home away from home. If you come in the summer, there's an ice cream parlor right across the road. They have the best ice cream in town."

– Sine Jensen

41 **Bæst**
Map C, P.103

The Italian eatery in Nørrebro, the third from chef Christian Puglisi, is famous for its sourdough pizzas, homemade charcuterie and mozzarellas. With a focus on quality meats, Bæst makes all its dishes from scratch, a reflection of Puglisi's cooking philosophy, which focuses on organic and locally sourced food. The restaurant has a large following. So book in advance, especially on weekends! If you're in the area in the morning, check out Mirabelle, a bakery adjoined to Bæst that sells fresh bread and pastries, as well as a "dish of the day" for take away.

🕐 1700-2230 daily
🏠 Guldbergsgade 29, 2200
📞 +45 3535 0463
URL baest.dk

"Try the burrata and their drinks! We're behind their graphic identity."

– Jack Dahl, Homework

42 Fiskebaren
Map I, P.107

Situated in the trendy Meatpacking district (#49), this world-renowned fish restaurant has a legion of followers who swear by their mouth-watering oysters. With a focus on locally sourced seafood, the concise menu offers artfully prepared dishes featuring simple yet pure flavours, as well as an selection of excellent cocktails. The Nordic-inspired interior, with its metallic surfaces, sleek white tiles and a 1,000-litre aquarium, sets a casual yet vibrant atmosphere. You can choose to sit at the bar, lounge on the sofas or relax at the tables but when summer arrives, the outdoor patio is a popular spot.

🕐 1730–0000 (Su–Th), –0200 (F–Sa)
🏠 Flæsketorvet 100, 1711
📞 +45 3215 5656 🔗 fiskebaren.dk

"This is my favourite place to eat fish. Reserve table in advance."

– Josephine Philip, Darkness Falls

43 Copenhagen Street Food
Map R, P.109

This temporary street food market, slated to reopen at another spot in 2018, is located on Papirøen (Paper Island) in a former newspaper-storage warehouse. In its raw, cavernous halls, you'll find a multitude of food trucks and stalls serving sustainable street food from all around the world. With a mandate to provide inexpensive, ethical and delicious meals, the market also functions as a creative hub for artists and musicians, and often hosts events, such as DJ sets and flea markets. If the weather's nice, enjoy your meal outside overlooking Copenhagen's harbour.

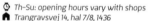

🕐 *Th–Su: opening hours vary with shops*
🏠 *Trangravsvej 14, hal 7/8, 1436*
📘 *Copenhagen Street Food – Papirøen*
🔗 *copenhagenstreetfood.dk* 🖉 *Market takes winter breaks from mid December to February.*

"This is the perfect place for lunch or a light supper but it can be rather crowded. You can find all types of cuisine, all offering high quality at a reasonable price."
– Line Rix, Kit Couture

077

44 Slotskælderen hos Gitte Kik
Map D, P.105

For a classic Danish lunch that's easy on the wallet, visit Slotskælderen, one of the best places in the city to try smørrebrød, a traditional open-faced sandwich prepared with toppings of the diner's choice, including pickled herring, smoked salmon, shrimp, as well as vegetarian options. Family run since 1910, the restaurant is housed in a cosy basement space that still retains its original rustic charm. Hot and cold dishes are also served. Located next to Christiansborg Palace (#17) and the Danish Parliament, this institution is a popular destination for politicians, so call ahead for reservations.

🕐 1000–1700 (Tu–Sa), 1100–1500 (M, Dec)
🏠 Fortunstræde 4, 1065 📞 +45 3311 1537
🔗 www.slotskælderen.dk
📎 Restaurant takes summer breaks and closes on all public holidays. Phone reservations only.

"Walk up to the counter and talk to your chef about what you like and what he recommends. Make sure to drink a cold beer to compliment your food."

– Casper Heijkenskjöld

45 Café Victor
Map D, P.105

Opening in 1981 as a French-inspired brasserie, Café Victor is the place to go to indulge in first-rate cuisine. Sophisticated dining is the goal here. Come for a glass of cold white wine and moules-frites or a plate of oysters, or simply grab a coffee and watch some of the city's wealthiest settle in for a meal. If you're craving comfort food, they also serve winning croque monsieur and Eggs Benedict. With a slight air of pretension, this café resembles a Parisian bistro, featuring small tables, brass fixtures and large windows along the front. If you want some breathing space, ask to be seated outdoors, where you can enjoy views of the cosy side streets in the city's central shopping district.

🕐 0800–0100 (M–W), –0200 (Th–F), 0900–0200 (Sa), 1100–0000 (Su)
🏠 Ny Østergade 8, 1101
📞 +45 3313 3613 🔗 cafevictor.dk

"It is a classic where you can meet old friends and enjoy traditional Danish/French food. It's always busy, so book a table in advance."

– Kim Herforth Nielsen, 3XN Architects

46 Relæ
Map C, P.102

Christian Puglisi's first restaurant is known for its no-fuss, wallet-friendly approach to fine dining and commitment to sustainability, but Relæ recently turned heads with its switch to two seatings per night. The minimalist interior – featuring plenty of wood and leather – keeps the focus on the plate. Expect simple and clean dishes with complex, carefully thought out flavours. Across the street is Relæ's sister restaurant, Manfreds, where you can also enjoy uncomplicated yet playful dishes focusing on organic produce.

🕐 1730-2130 (W-Th), 1200-1330, 1730-2200 (F-Sa)
🏠 Jægersborggade 41, 2200
☎ +45 3696 6609
🌐 www.restaurant-relae.dk

"The food looks simple, but then taste and intellectual reflections appear in layers. If you want a full treat, ask for both vegetarian and normal menu..."

– Jakob Mielcke, Mielcke & Hurtigkarl

47 Kadeau

Map M, P.108

Founded by two childhood friends, Nicolai Nørregaard and Rasmus Kofoed, who were later joined by Magnus Kofoed, this nature-inspired restaurant started on the small island of Bornholm. After words spread to the capital, the team opened another restaurant, this time on the island of Christianshavn. Their inventive use of locally sourced food helped them earn their first Michelin star in 2013. If you have time, go for the full menu "borholmer-bank" – a series of 20 small servings for around US$235. Likes its food, Kadeau's interior, with its custom-made furniture and wooden detailing, takes its cues from the nature of Bornholm.

🕐 1830–2000 (M–F), 1200–1300, 1830–2000 (Sa)
🏠 Wildersgade 10b, 1408   📞 +45 3325 2223
URL kadeau.dk

"Visit their Bornholm restaurant if you can. The trip will take 4 hours by bus or ferry from Copenhagen through Sweden."

– Marie Louise Munkegaard

48 Stedsans – CleanSimpleLocal
Map O, P.109

Set in the middle of a 600 square-metre organic rooftop farm built five floors above a former car-auction building, Stedsans – Clean-SimpleLocal is run by food entrepreneur Mette Helbæk and her husband. Using only local, organic produce, the seasonal restaurant serves its meals "family style" – shared among diners who are seated at a long table located in the farm's greenhouse. With a clear view of the stars when the sun sets, this unique dining experience combines the serenity of nature with clean and simple food. Be sure to subscribe to their newsletter to find out when a spot opens as reservations can fill up months ahead.

🕒 💲 *Seating at 1730: kr 695, 2015: kr 845 (Th-Su, Apr-Oct)* 🏠 *Rooftop, Æbeløgade 4, 2100*
🔗 *www.cleansimplelocal.com*
🔖 *Dress warm for inclement weather.*

"*Everything, from the location to the food and the wine is extraordinary. It's an unforgettable and intimate experience that lasts at least a few hours.*"
– Esteban

Nightlife

Classic cocktails, low key bars and micro-breweries

The cocktail scene in Copenhagen is growing as players get more inventive. The drinks are not cheap but you can find quality ones in almost any area of the city. A few of the best cocktail bars also serve excellent food, such as Salon 39 (#59) in Frederiksberg. If wine is what you're looking for, you won't go hungry or thirsty at 20a (#56) in Nørrebro, Beer and the art of brewing is also serious business in Copenhagen, with Mikkeller (#60) is leading the way. They opened their first beer bar in Viktoriagade and now run several around the city.

Later at night, for dancing into the early hours, hit up the Meatpacking District (#49) or consider Vega, a popular venue for music and drinks, but also an architectural gem created by Vilhelm Lauritzen in the 1950s as a meeting hall for the Danish workers union. For live music, head to Culture Box, an electronic music venue, or try Rust, known for featuring up-and-coming artists from a variety of genres, including hip-hop, dancehall and indie-rock.

Summer is festival season in Copenhagen. Kicking it off is Distortion, usually with a huge final party at Refshaleøen (#52), then Roskilde Festival, the Copenhagen Jazz Festival and later in August, there are some smaller events, including Søndagsvenner, Uhørt, Strøm and Stella Polaris.

Andreas M Hansen
Multidisciplinary designer

I specialise in brand identity, web design, art direction and calligraphy. I'm the Head of Design at software company Airtame in my hometown, Copenhagen.

Lidkoeb
P.090

Jakob Kahlen
Creative director, B&O PLAY

As a Global Creative Director, I'm building Bang & Olufsen's rebel child into a lifestyle audio brand fit for urban creatives. My work bridges product design, branding and marketing.

Le Gammeltoft
Founder, Heartbeats

Le Gammeltoft's heart beats for creativity and music. She's a DJ and owner of Heartbeats Radio, record label SOUND OF COPEN-HAGEN and Bar O, and has lived in Copenhagen her whole life.

Kødbyen
P.088

Bar O
P.091

Louise Brandstrup Zastrow, *dot the i*

I'm a writer, editor, trendspotter, mother and wife. I run dot the i, a micro-global studio and consultancy that guides decision makers on brand, communication and design strategy.

Llama
P.094

Lars Larsen
Founder, Kilo Design

Lars Larsen founded design agency Kilo and co-created KiBiSi with Bjarke Ingels and Jens Martin Skibsted. He's known for having a natural eye for simple solutions to complex design challenges.

Vibe Lundemark
Designer, Tabernacle Twins

With a MA from Royal College of Art, London, I design expressive prints and knits for Danish womenswear label Tabernacle Twins.

Refshaleøen
P.092

GILT
P.095

Phong Phan
Co-founder, HEAVY

Phong Phan is a Danish designer who creates visual narratives imbued with Scandinavian simplicity. He co-founded design and branding agency HEAVY with Robert Daniel Nagy.

Hansens Gamle Familiehave
P.096

20a
P.097

Maria Bruun
Furniture designer

Maria Bruun works at the interface of design, architecture and art. She has a love for authenticity and honest experiences, both in her work and her daily life.

Christian Grosen Rasmussen, *MUUTO*

I was born and raised in Copenhagen and live with my wife and kids in Frederiksberg. I'm an architect and the Design Director at Danish interior brand, MUUTO.

Salon 39
P.098

Nathalie Schwer
Interior stylist

I travel a lot for work and pleasure. When I'm not working, I enjoy walking my dog and hanging out with my friends and family. This guide reflects how I use the city myself.

Bo-bi Bar
P.099

Mikkeller Bar
P.100

Femmes Régionales
Creative agency

Mie Albæk Nielsen and Caroline Hansen founded Femmes Régionales, a creative agency that offers complete communication and marketing solutions for fashion and lifestyle clients.

Elias Bender Rønnenfelt
Lead singer, Iceage

Elias Bender Rønnenfelt is one-fourth of Copenhagen punk rock band, Iceage.

Mayhem
P.101

49 Kødbyen

Map I, P.107

Food and meat are still sold to businesses in the area, but an increasing number of bars, clubs and restaurants are taking over. Since 1995, when the city declared the district protected for its 1930s functionalist architecture, Copenhagen's Meatpacking District has turned into one big party. Whatever you're in the mood for, you can find it here: Tommi's Burger Joint for comfort food, Warpigs for BBQ or NOHO for cocktails. For clubbing, head to Bakken or Jolene. To get your culture fix, visit any number of galleries, such as V1 or Bo Bjerregaard, or visit Nibble, a food-themed book and magazine shop run by the guys behind I'm a KOMBO and Restaurant Congo.

🏠 Kødbyen, 1711

URL www.burgerjoint.dk, warpigs.dk, noho.bar, www.bakkenkbh.dk, www. istedgrill.dk, www.v1gallery.com, www.nibbleshop.com

"When you've had enough alcohol, head 100 metres up to Isted Grill at Istedgade 92. Here you will find the best roast pork sandwich you have ever tried."

– Andreas M Hansen

BioMio (above), V1 Gallery, Nimble (below)

50 Lidkoeb
Map H, P.107

Serving up some of the best cocktails in town since 2012, Lidkoeb is a popular venue among locals looking to relax on the weekends. The owners also run the exclusive Ruby cocktail bar, but its sister location has a slightly more rebellious air, featuring louder music. While maintaining the same laid-back atmosphere, Lidkoeb is larger, with ample seating stretching over three floors of an elegancy restored 18th-century building nestled in a back alley off Vesterbrogade. Featuring the classics, as well as house creations, Lidkoeb recently expanded with a small whiskey bar on the top floor.

🕐 1600–0200 (M–Sa), 2000– (Su)
🏠 Vesterbrogade 72B, 1620
📞 +45 3311 2010 **URL** lidkoeb.dk

"If you get there early and you're lucky, you might get seated in the classic Spanish chairs by the fireplace."

– Jakob Kahlen, B&O PLAY

51 Bar O

Map D, P.105

Owned by two of Denmark's most famous DJs, Peter Visti and Le Gammeltoft, Bar O is known for great cocktails and music alike. After midnight, the bar transforms into a club, creating an intimate atmosphere for dancing into the early hours. One of the owners is always behind the DJ counter, building the party from start to finish. From the obscure to the mainstream, the music sets meld pulsing electronic beats with smooth renditions of disco hits, a reflection of Visti and Le Gammeltoft's diverse tastes. Open only two nights a week — Fridays and Saturdays – with no fixed closing hour.

🕐 2100 till late (F–Sa)
🏠 Pilestræde 12, 1112
URL www.barocph.dk

"Peter Visti is known for his love for music and it is this passion that drives Bar O."

– Le Gammeltoft, Heartbeats

52 Refshaleøen
Map L, P.108

Once home to one of the world's largest shipyards, the former industrial site has reinvented itself as a cultural retreat of sorts. From Michelin-starred Amass to theatre collective Asterions Hus, you'll find plenty to do on this historic island, which also serves as venue for summer music festivals, such as Distortion and Søndagsvenner. If you're looking to unwind, head over to Halvandet beach or the recently opened skateboard park that offers fantastic views of the city. A weekend flea market known for its huge collections of 1960s Danish designer furniture takes place every two weeks.

f Refshaleøen **URL** refshaleoen.dk
*@ www.amassrestaurant.com,
www.asterionshus.dk, www.cphdistortion.dk*

"Walk among the massive buildings in this run-down shipyard and you might spot treasures that are yet to be uncovered. It also boasts the city's greatest view!"

– Louise Brandstrup Zastrow, dot the i

Amass (above), Distortion (below)

53 Llama
Map D, P.105

Part of the Cofoco's chain of trendy-yet-affordable restaurants, Llama was one of the first in the city to draw on the flavours of South America and Mexico. Its menu features ceviches, anticuchos, tacos – all rooted in Scandinavian culinary tradition – with local ingredients used whenever possible. Its lively interior, filled with colourful Mexican tiles and brass light fixtures, conjures a subtle Latin vibe without all the gimmicks. With two seatings per evening, its large dining space can fit 180 guests and an even bigger crowd on weekend club nights, making this a loud, vibrant establishment teeming with energy.

🕐 1800–0030 (Su-Th), –0300 (F-Sa)
🏠 Lille Kongensgade 14, 1074
📞 +45 8993 6687 ⓕ Llama Restaurant & Bar
🔗 llamarestaurant.dk

"Book a late table Friday or Saturday and stay all night for party, DJ and cocktails."

– Lars Larsen, Kilo Design

 54 **GILT**
Map C, P.102

Opening the bar in 2003, when the city had virtually no cocktail scene, owner Peter Altenburg is credited with helping Copenhagen gain international recognition. With a welcoming atmosphere and dedication to quality, GILT serves up classic cocktails – with a Nordic twist. Locally foraged elderflower, rhubarb and buckthorn are often used in their drinks, expertly prepared by knowledgeable bartenders who are more than willing to take requests outside their seasonally adapted menu. Dim

lights and a dark façade set a relaxing tone. Short for Glass, Ice, Liqueur and Topping, GILT is for grown-ups looking for sophistication.

🕐 1800-0100 (W-Th), -0200 (F-Sa)
🏠 Rantzausgade 39, 2200
📞 +45 2726 8070
📘 Gilt Cocktailbar 🌐 gilt.dk

"This is the coolest cocktail bar in Copenhagen. You get swept away immediately when entering this hidden treasure."

– Vibe Lundemark, Tabernacle Twins

55 Hansens Gamle Familiehave

Map E, P.106

This family garden restaurant has managed to capture the very essence of traditional Danish food, served in a friendly and cosy environment. Dating back to the 1850s, Hansens Gamle Familiehave originally sold coffee and tea to high society strolling through the Frederiksberg Gardens. Today, the menu includes open-faced sandwiches, fresh salads and classic warm dishes, such as *biksemad* (Danish hash), that vary according to the season. Consider having a cold beer or schnapps, which many consider a must with these dishes.

🕐 Jan-Mar, Oct-Dec 22: 1100-2400 (Tu-Sa), -1800 (Su), Apr-Sep: 1100-2400 daily
🏠 Pile Allé 10-12, 2000
📞 +45 3630 9257 🔗 hansenshave.dk
🖉 Opening hours may vary by year

"*Schnapps and herring together are mandatory. Get Jubilæums Akvavit if you want something relatively mild in taste.*"

– Phong Phan, HEAVY

 56 20a
Map C, P.103

Mainly a wine bar with a menu that changes
from day to day, 20a offers a hot daily dish,
classic charcuterie and a great selection of
cheese. The cuisine is mainly French-inspired,
but you'll also find Mediterranean and Nordic
influences. In the summer, take advantage
of the outdoor seating, where you can easily
while away the warm evenings with a lovely
glass of wine. Unlike many other restaurants
in Copenhagen, 20a is also open on Mondays.
They also own two other establishments – 18 in
Østerbro and Sankt Annæ 8 on Christianshavn
– but 20a has the largest selection of wine.

🕐 1700–0000 (M–F), 1300– (Sa)
🏠 Ravnsborggade 20A, 2200
📞 +45 2597 4601
URL www.20a.dk

*"20a is an amazing wine bar! The atmosphere and
very homey service, food and pricing is supreme."*
– Maria Bruun

 57 Salon 39
Map B, P.102

Located next to The Lakes and the planetarium, Salon 39 offers cocktails you won't find anywhere else, as well as the classics. Its charming library-like interior and delectable dinner menu make it the perfect setting for a casual yet intimate dining experience. The excellent and creative bartenders are into whiskey and bourbons, but they also carry special gins and other liqueurs imported from around the world. Get their recommendations or simply let them surprise you. The space is tiny, so come early if you want a table.

🕐 1600–2330 (M–W), –0030 (Th), –0130 (F–Sa),
Kitchen: 1730–2200 daily
🏠 Vodroffsvej 39, 1900
📞 +45 3920 8039
URL www.salon39.dk

"Their bartenders are the best and mix some of the best cocktails in the city. You can also have dinner there."

– Christian Grosen Rasmussen, MUUTO

58 Bo-bi Bar
Map D, P.105

Bo-bi is rumoured to be the first American-style bar in Copenhagen, opened in 1917 by a sailor returning home from New York. Since then, it's been a favourite among those looking for cold bottled beer and conversations with strangers. Sourced mainly from a small brewery in Fynen, beer is served everyday from noon to 2 a.m. Most of its interior, with its red lamps and wallpaper, hasn't changed since the beginning. Important to note: this is one of a few bars in Copenhagen where smoking is still allowed inside. Make sure to get a hardboiled egg as your late night snack!

🕐 1200-0200 (Su–F), -0000 (Sa)
🏠 Klareboderne 14, 1115
📞 +45 3312 5543

"This is a traditional Danish bar where you get cheap beer and hang out with artist, writers and everyone else. Nowhere else can get better than this."

– Nathalie Schwer

59 Mikkeller Bar
Map H, P.107

One of the most admired names among the craft-beer aficionados, Mikkeller was founded by two home brewers who turned a hobby into an internationally renown company. At their first bar in Viktoriagade, you'll find a rotating selection of 20 taps from their own brewery and others around the world. They also serve a small selection of their own spirits. Gourmet cheese and cured meats are also available, but go next door to Mikkeller's own restaurant Øl & Brød (Beer and Bread) for gourmet open-faced sandwiches, if you're looking for a meal. Mikkeller also has establishments in Nørrebro and Kødbyen.

🕐 1300–0100 (Su–W), –0200 (Th–F), 1200– (Sa)
🏠 Viktoriagade 8 B–C, 1655
📞 +45 3331 0415 ⬛ Mikkeller
URL mikkeller.dk

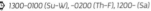

"Mikkeller is probably one of Copenhagen's best brewers. If you meet someone nice here, buy them a beer and ask them to teach you how to say cheers in Danish."

– Mie Albæk Nielsen & Caroline Hansen, Femmes Régionales

60 Mayhem
Map N, P.109

This non-profit showspace has been hosting the stranger and more uncompromising sides of Copenhagen music for the last few years, as well art shows, poetry readings and the occasional movie screening. Run by volunteers in the artistic community, Mayhem can be a challenge to actually find, ensconced behind graffiti-covered walls on the outskirts of the city in the semi-lawless area Ragnhildgade 1. A venue for great live music, expect to hear an eclectic mix of experimental sounds from underground artists. Opening hours are limited, so check the website for event details.

🕐 💲 *Showtime & admission vary with programmes*
🏠 *Ragnhildgade 1, 2100*
URL *www.mayhemkbh.dk*

"I'm proud to be part of the warehouse. Going on the right night might result in some very special encounters with sights and sounds you ever seen and heard."

– Elias Bender Rønnenfelt, Iceage

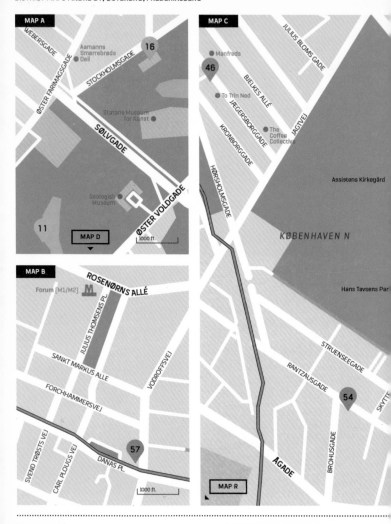

- 11_Botanisk Have
- 16_Den Hirschsprungske Samling
- 46_Relæ
- 54_GILT
- 57_Salon 39

- 19_Limited Works
- 37_Kaffebar
- 41_Bæst
- 56_20a

Super Bikeways

- 7_Dronningegården
- 10_Rundetårn
- 14_Kunstforeningen GL STRAND
- 15_Etage Projects
- 17_Christiansborg Slot
- 21_Thorvaldsens Museum
- 25_HAY HOUSE
- 26_Schäfer Grafisk Værksted
- 27_Format Artspace
- 28_Cinnober
- 30_Storm

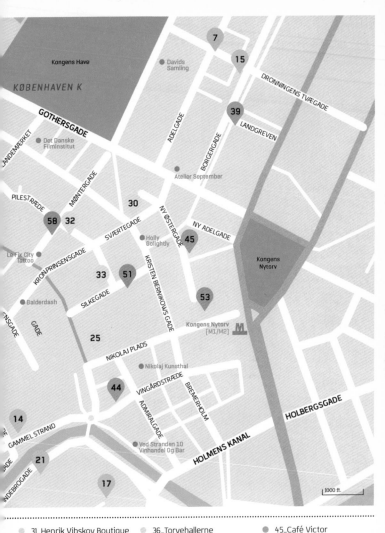

KØBENHAVN K

Kongens Have

Davids Samling

DRONNINGENS TVÆGADE

GOTHERSGADE

LANDEMÆRKET

Det Danske Filminstitut

ADELGADE

BORGERGADE

LANDGREVEN

MØNTERGADE

PILESTRÆDE

Atelier September

30

NY ØSTERGADE

SVÆRTEGADE

NY ADELGADE

58 32

Le-Fix City Tattoo

KRONPRINSENSGADE

Holly Golightly

45

Kongens Nytorv

33 51

KRISTEN BERNIKOWS GADE

Balderdash

SILKEGADE

53

SGADE

GADE

25

Kongens Nytorv
[M1/M2] M

NIKOLAJ PLADS

Nikolaj Kunsthal

44

VINGÅRDSTRÆDE

BREMERHOLM

14

ADMIRALGADE

HOLBERGSGADE

GAMMEL STRAND

21

Ved Stranden 10
Vinhandel Og Bar

HOLMENS KANAL

INDEBROGADE

17

1000 ft.

DISTRICT MAPS : **FREDERIKSBERG, ISLANDS BRYGGE, VESTERBRO**

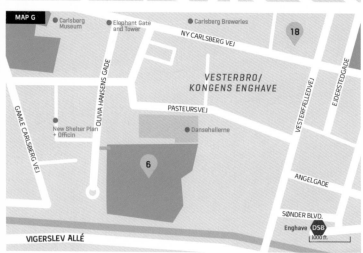

- ● 4_Kalvebod Bølge
- ● 6_J.C. Jacobsens Have
- ● 18_Galleri Nicolai Wallner & Nils Stærk
- ● 38_Alimentari
- ● 55_Hansens Gamle Familiehave

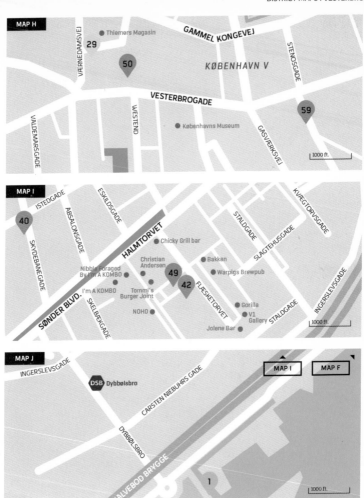

- 1_Cykelslangen
- 29_Playtype Store
- 40_Sort Kaffe & Vinyl
- 42_Fiskebaren
- 49_Kødbyen
- 50_Lidkoeb
- 59_Mikkeller Bar

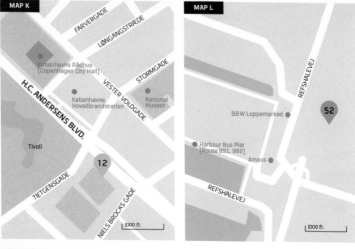

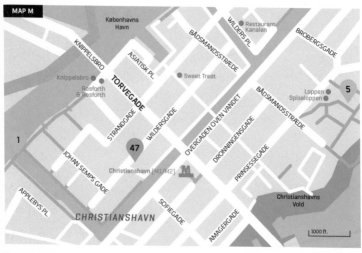

- 1_Cirkelbroen
- 5_Christiania
- 12_Glyptoteket
- 47_Kadeau
- 52_Refshaleøen

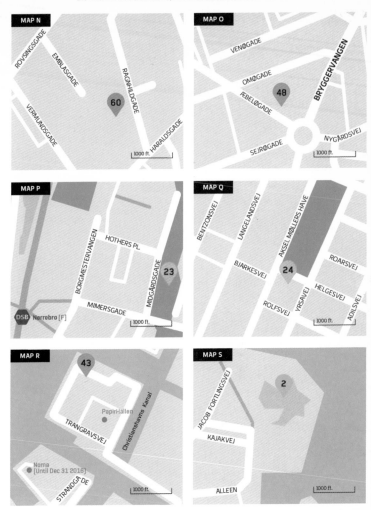

- ● 2_Den Blå Planet
- ● 23_Superkilen
- ● 24_Frederiksberg Svøm-mehal
- ● 43_Copenhagen Street Food
- ● 48_Stedsans – CleanSimpleLocal
- ● 60_Mayhem

DISTRICT MAPS : **DRONNINGMØLLE, HELSINGØR, HUMLEBÆK, CHARLOTTENLUND, BAGSVAERD, BISPEBJERG**

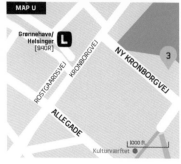

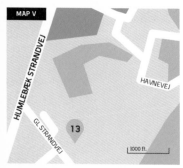

- 3_Museet for Søfart
- 8_Bagsværd Kirke
- 9_Grundtvigs Kirke
- 13_Louisiana Museum of Modern Art
- 20_Finn Juhls hus
- 22_Rudolph Tegners Museum

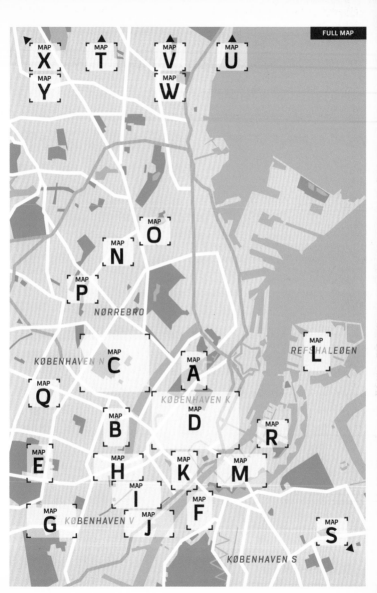

Accommodation

Hip hostels, fully-equipped apartments & swanky hotels

No journey is perfect without a good night's sleep to recharge. Whether you're backpacking or on a business trip, our picks combine top quality and convenience, whatever your budget.

 <kr800   kr801–1600   >kr1601+

Urban House Copenhagen

Fun activity spaces, cosy communal areas and a live stage set in a warm industrial interior, Urban House offers guests a dynamic social life while maintaining efficient service with neat basic rooms and friendly staff on standby 24/7. A tattoo parlour and bike rental are available in-house to add up to a hip Vesterbro experience, while Copenhagen Central Station is right behind.

🏠 Colbjørnsensgade 5-11, 1652
📞 +45 3323 2929 🔲 urbanhouse.me $)

Hotel SP34

A boutique hotel distinct for its sleek Scandinavian interior, SP34 blends in well with the vintage fashion stores, chic cafés and bars in the old Latin Quarter. In addition to two restaurants serving gourmet tapas and homemade burgers, the hotel also pampers guests with a free glass of wine between 5–6pm every day.

🏠 *Sankt Peders Stræde 34, 1453*
📞 *+45 3313 3000* 🔗 *www.brochner-hotels.dk/locations/hotel-sp34*

Charlottehaven

Beautifully complemented by a lush courtyard, Charlottehaven is a hotel apartment complex with a gym, beauty clinic and child care centre. The Lundgaard & Tranberg Arkitekter-designed building houses a homey setting, with separate bedrooms and living rooms and fully equipped kitchens in each apartment, while keeping a 24-hour reception.

🏠 Hjørringgade 12C, 2100 📞 +45 3527 1500 💲
🔗 www.charlottehaven.com

STAY

🏠 Islands Brygge 79A, 2300
☎ +45 7244 4434
🔗 staycopenhagen.dk

Generator Copenhagen

🏠 Adelgade 5-7, 1304
☎ +45 7877 5400
🔗 generatorhostels.com/en/
destinations/copenhagen

Central Hotel og Café

🏠 Tullinsgade 1, 1610
☎ +45 33 21 00 95
🔗 www.centralhotelogcafe.dk

Notes

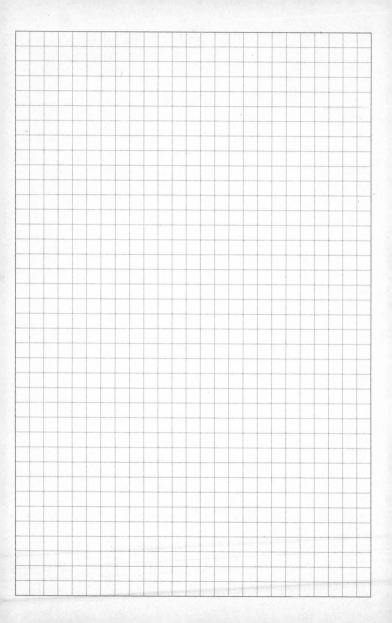

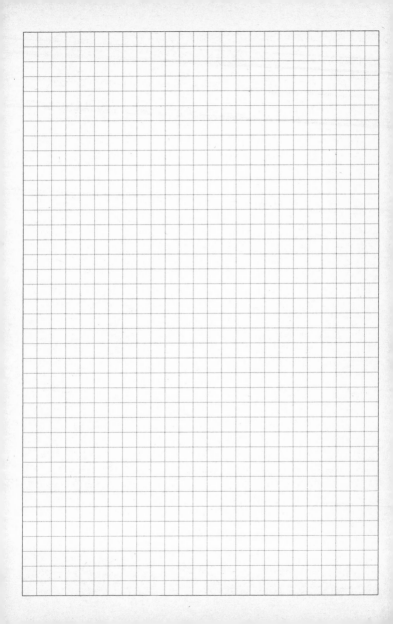